Air Assault Teams

by Gerard Stapleton

Capstone Press

MINNEAPOLIS

Printed in the United States of America.

Capstone Press • 2440 Fernbrook Lane • Minneapolis, MN 55447

Editorial Director   John Coughlan
Managing Editor   Tom Streissguth
Production Editor   James Stapleton
Book Design   Timothy Halldin

Library of Congress Cataloging-in-Publication Data

Stapleton, Gerard, 1971-
    Air assault teams / by Gerard Stapleton.
      p. cm. -- (Serving your country)
    Includes bibliographical references and index.
    Summary: Describes the history, major battles, and training necessary to become a member of the Army's 101st Airborne Division.
    ISBN 1-56065-285-3
    1. United States. Army. Airborne Division, 101st-- Juvenile literature. [1. United States. Army. Airborne Division, 101st.]
    I. Title. II. Series.
    UA27.5 101st.S73 1995
    356'.166'0973--dc20   95-21410
                                                    CIP
                                                    AC

Table of Contents

Chapter 1

"Nuts"

The 101st Airborne Division has a long history, going all the way back to World War I. The "Screaming Eagles" of the 101st have won victories in World War II, the Vietnam War, and Operation Desert Storm.

The men and women of the 101st hold a wide variety of ranks and responsibilities. Grease monkeys fix and maintain all the **division's** equipment. Instructors of the Air Assault School teach each soldier how to jump

Air assault teams gather at a landing site during an operation in the Central American nation of Panama.

from a speeding aircraft and how to rappel to the ground from a hovering helicopter. Together, the members of the 101st Airborne Division make up a proud and able family.

"Nuts"

Late in 1944, near the end of World War II (1939-1945), German leaders targeted the French town of Bastogne. This surprise attack was part of a bigger operation called the Battle

Paratroopers practice an assault from a World War II glider. Hundreds of gliders were used during the Normandy invasion.

of the Bulge. Important fuel dumps and a center for Allied communications lay between Bastogne and another town, St. Vith.

General Dwight D. Eisenhower decided that Bastogne must be held at all costs. The 101st Airborne was ordered to the area. By December 19th, the division was dug in around the town. By the 21st, two German divisions had completely surrounded the 101st.

The weather did not permit the Army to parachute in relief supplies. Confident of winning, a German party under a flag of truce demanded that the 101st surrender. General McAuliffe, the division commander, responded "nuts!" Word of this courageous response swept through the division.

On Christmas Day, the gunners, cooks, drivers, and clerks of the 101st bravely fought to hold off a major German attack. Gradually the Germans advanced. Finally, in early January, Lieutenant-General George Patton arrived with the 3rd U.S. Tank Division. The counterattack drove the Germans from Bastogne. To honor their heroism, the president awarded the 101st the Presidential Unit Citation. It was the first time an entire division had won this medal.

A screaming eagle is part of the official insignia of the 101st Airborne Division.

Chapter 2

The History of the 101st Airborne

The 101st Division formed in July 1918 to
fight in France in World War I (1914-1918).
After the war ended, the division became a
reserve unit headquartered in Milwaukee,
Wisconsin.

In 1940 the U.S. Army activated the first
airborne combat unit. After two years, the army
formed two airborne divisions–the 101st
Airborne Division and the 82nd Airborne

**Members of the 101st jump from a C-130 plane
during an exercise.**

Division. These divisions did not have large numbers of men, heavy weapons, or tanks. Instead, the soldiers trained to strike quickly in enemy territory.

The new divisions had small support teams, parachute units, and glider units. Gliders were planes with no engines that could drop supplies and paratroopers. Later, other units were

Helicopter assaults were more common than high-altitude drops in the dense jungles of Vietnam.

assigned to the division, making it unlike any other combat unit.

Many commanders did not understand the abilities of the new division. Often, they failed to give the 101st enough support for dangerous missions. But the 101st made up for the lack of supplies with courage and bravery. Nevertheless, the unit suffered heavy losses throughout World War II.

The 101st Airborne continued to change after World War II. In Vietnam the division became the 101st Airborne (Airmobile) Division. Its members no longer parachuted out of planes. On October 4, 1974 the official name of the unit changed to the 101st Airborne Division (Air Assault).

Since the Vietnam War (1964-1975), Air Assault Teams have trained and served in many different places, from the Egyptian desert to the cold Arctic. Their last major operation was in the Persian Gulf War in 1991, when the United States and its allies fought Iraq, a small Middle Eastern country.

Chapter 3

Battles and Missions

D-Day

On the night of June 5, 1944, 6,000 101st Airborne soldiers made the first jump on D-Day–the World War II Allied invasion of western Europe. Their mission was to link Utah and Omaha beaches, two attack points for the invasion into France. The massive paratrooper drop would help the U.S. and its allies take the Germans by surprise.

Troops swarm ashore during the D-Day landings of June 6, 1944.

World War II paratroopers prepare to land behind enemy lines.

The 101st had to protect a path for the 4th **Infantry** Division, which would be landing on the beaches in a few hours. The 4th Infantry Division had to march south from Utah beach to link with troops marching inland from Omaha beach.

After making their jump, the paratroopers were scattered over a wide and dangerous territory. Some men drowned after drifting out to sea. Others jumped dangerously close to the ground.

Despite heavy losses, about 2,500 paratroopers still managed to assemble with their equipment. Nine days after the drop, and through fierce battles, the 101st linked with the 82nd Airborne. And by clearing a path for the troops of the 4th Infantry, the 101st accomplished its mission.

Post-War Reorganizations

After World War II, the army shaped the 101st into several different formations. The division was deactivated three times. In September 1956, the 101st again became an active unit at Fort Campbell, Kentucky.

In 1964, the 101st was converted into a ROAD (Reorganization Objective Army Division) unit. A variety of flexible **battalions** made up the division. Their organization would depend on the units involved and on the particular mission. This idea would be very successful in Vietnam.

The Nomads of Vietnam

The 101st Airborne Division's 1st **Brigade** entered the Republic of Vietnam on July 29, 1965. From 1965 to 1974, the U.S. fought against the Communist North Vietnamese. For

more than two years, the 1st Brigade traveled 2,500 miles and fought in 26 different operations. Its members earned the nickname of Nomads of Vietnam.

A cargo plane drops a troop carrier. Airborne units must know how to parachute heavy equipment.

The remaining parts of the 101st Division arrived in November 1967. Each battalion formed reconnaissance **platoons** to gather information. These platoons were skilled in patrol and ambush.

In Vietnam, the 101st Airborne used helicopters instead of airplanes. There was no need for large parachute assaults like those used in World War II. As a result, fewer members of the 101st were qualified to jump. This changed the division name to the 101st Airborne (Air Mobile) Division. This unit was transported all over Vietnam to help fight at trouble spots. Ap Bia Mountain, also known as Hamburger Hill, was a famous battlefield where the 101st suffered heavy losses.

Cobra

During the 1991 Gulf War, the main mission of the 101st was to clear a path between Baghdad, Iraq and Kuwait. In order to accomplish this mission, the unit set up a large **FOB (forward operating base)** 50 miles inside of Iraq. The military code-named this point Cobra. It would be used as jump-off point for the invasion of Iraq.

A week before the operation, UH60 Apache helicopters began attacking Iraqi bunkers. At

An air assault team moves to a forward location during Operation Desert Storm.

one site, an infantry unit captured over 400 prisoners. The prisoners revealed that Iraq had built several other troop bunkers and air defense sites. These sites would have caused heavy casualties. They would have helped Iraq stop the ground troops from reaching Cobra.

An artillery battery launches a surface-to-air missile.
Airborne divisions also include heavy weaponry.

A Classic Airborne Problem

The 187th Infantry Brigade–part of the
101st Division–was facing attack from all
sides. The brigade sat north of FOB Cobra.
Their mission was to stop any Iraqi troops
marching south toward Cobra.

But bad weather slowed them down. Winter
rains brought thick fog and mud. Anti-tank

units and support helicopters could not make it to their position. The infantry soldiers were left sitting in the cold desert, without support, waiting for an Iraqi attack.

A few vehicles were captured at the roadblocks, but no major attack took place. The rest of the brigade landed the night of the 26th. They bombed roads, blew up bridges, and set traps for enemy troops. The work of the brigade was important in the swift defeat of Iraq.

Chapter 4

Joining the Army

If you are between the ages of 17 and 34, you can enter the armed forces. If you are under 18 years of age, your parents or guardian must give their permission.

Before making the oath to defend the United States, a future army soldier must decide how long to enlist. You may sign up for two, four, or six years of active service. No matter what you decide, you are actually joining for eight years. After active duty, soldiers join the

Mechanics repair a helicopter rotor blade.

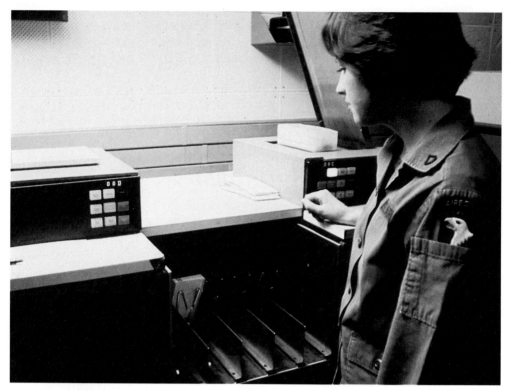

A member of the 101st Airborne checks a high-tech system.

inactive reserve. In case of war, the army may call up a reservist for active duty.

Army **recruiters** and high school counselors will help you with the decision to enlist. The **Armed Services Vocational Aptitude Battery (ASVAB)** test and high school grades will help you decide which military jobs best fit your talents.

An army soldier may volunteer to join the 101st Airborne Division (Air Assault). After completing **basic training** and Advanced Individual Training (AIT), a soldier can request to attend Air Assault School.

Once there, after you pass a tough 11-day trial, you may join the 101st Airborne (Air Assault) Division.

Airborne troops relax during a mission in the Middle Eastern nation of Saudi Arabia.

Chapter 5

Air Assault School

The fear of falling down a 34-foot wall, or dropping 100 feet to the ground, are the least of your worries at Air Assault School. The training is physically tough, and trainees must master dozens of technical procedures and life-saving techniques. Highly trained instructors help students learn skills and build confidence.

Each class begins with 170 students. The students come from various other special units of the armed forces, including the Green Berets and Army Rangers. Since Air Assault School

Troops rappel from a chopper during training exercises.

opened in January 1974, more than 90,000 U.S. and foreign soldiers have passed through the school. The 11-day camp includes combat assault, rigging and slinging loads, and rappelling.

Combat Assault

The combat assault part of the school teaches different combat-assault techniques. Trainees learn to work safely around all types of helicopters. They work in teams to set up landing zones and perform medical evacuation. Training takes place both day and night, just as in real combat situations. In their final exercise, students carry out a night combat assault using UH-60A Blackhawk helicopters.

Rigging and Slinging Loads

Rigging and slinging means to tie and secure something using rope. In this section, students learn to prepare and rig different equipment to be suspended from the belly of a helicopter. There is one night exercise and two day exercises using the huge CH-47 Chinook helicopter.

For the final test, an instructor slings a piece of equipment incorrectly under a helicopter. The student must identify three out of

A powerful Blackhawk chopper lifts a Humvee from the ground.

every four rigging mistakes and correct them. The helicopter must then take off and land again with no problems.

Students must remember a huge amount of information to pass this section. That is why many believe it is the toughest part of Air Assault School.

Rappelling

Rappel means to lower oneself to the ground using a rope. Soldiers rappel from helicopters into wooded or difficult terrain where a helicopter can not land. Starting at a12-foot (3.7-meter) wall, Air Assault students learn the basic rappelling techniques. The 34-foot (10.4-meter) wall comes next.

Here, instructors teach the Australian rappel, in which the student rappels down frontwards. In case of a mistake or a slip, the student usually ends up smashing head-first into the wall and hanging upside down.

The final exercise takes place 90 feet (27.5 meters) above the ground aboard a UH-60A helicopter. The student must use everything that he or she has learned. Errors may lead to serious injury or death. If a rope is misplaced, it may get caught in the helicopter rotor blades and send the whole crew crashing to the ground.

The final tests at Air Assault School demand physical stamina. The first rappel is done with combat gear. The second rappel is performed with a full pack and rifle, which weigh an extra 50 to 100 pounds (22.7 to 45.4 kilograms). For the final test, students must finish a 12-mile (19.2-kilometer) march in full field combat gear in under three hours.

Physical training is an important part of everyday life in the military.

Chapter 6

Air Assault

If the 101st Airborne is called into action, one-third of the entire unit can fly in a single helicopter lift within 48 hours. The division can transport its own weapons and equipment. Each soldier works in a team, helping the 101st to move quickly and efficiently.

The infantry of the 101st Airborne (Air Assault) Division includes the 327th, 502nd, and 187th infantry **regiments**. In each of these regiments are three infantry brigades. These units are each backed up by three other brigades: division **artillery**, the aviation brigade, and the division support command. On every mission the same aviation units work with the same infantry brigades. This system helps the teams coordinate their actions.

Grunts, Cannon Cockers, and Duck Hunters

The three infantry brigades are supported by a three-battalion artillery brigade and a separate Air Defense Artillery Battalion. There are three rifle companies of infantry soldiers, or "grunts." A special fourth **company** has 20 Humvees–rugged four-wheel-drive utility

Airborne troops prepare for an operation while the crew maneuvers its chopper into place.

trucks that help the infantry make quick attacks and retreats.

The artillery brigade uses heavy, long-range weapons. The artillery's latest gun is the M119 105mm British-made howitzer. This gun has a range of 9 miles (14,300 meters)–about 150 football fields.

Artillery soldiers (called cannon cockers) either perform a raid or make an attack. In a raid, the soldiers, a gun, and a Humvee are air-dropped to a spot, where they open fire on the target. During the raid, the Humvee allows the unit to maneuver on its own after landing. After the raid, a helicopter quickly picks up the unit.

The air-defense soldiers, called duckhunters, must protect the division's aircraft. Their weaponry includes Stinger shoulder-launched **surface-to-air missiles**. These missiles do not have to be fired directly at the target. Instead, they will lock onto the heat of an enemy aircraft's engine exhaust.

A soldier from the 101st surveys terrain in the Middle East.

Aviation Brigade

The aviation brigade includes a powerful fleet of 348 modern helicopters. These include the UH-64 Apache attack helicopter, the UH-60A Blackhawk troop transport, and the powerful CH-47 Chinook, which can carry heavy weapons and Humvees. An air cavalry squadron scouts ahead for the Apaches.

Three battalions fly the AH-64 Apache attack helicopters. These have laser-guided tracking and targeting systems that can hit targets during daylight or at night. A **forward-looking**

infrared sensor (FLIR) gives the pilot a "window" to see through the darkness.

The UH-60A Blackhawk performs a wide variety of duties. It can land 11 fully equipped infantry soldiers. Most often, the Blackhawk carries artillery, vehicles, and fuel and ammunition containers. The Blackhawk's laser-directed Hellfire missiles can destroy enemy tanks from 4 miles (6.4 kilometers) away.

CH-47 Chinooks are twin-bladed helicopters that can lift 3,000 pounds of heavy cargo. These powerful helicopters can carry a

Airborne units use converted Humvees as ambulance vehicles.

The Apache helicopter is one of the fastest and deadliest air weapons in the world.

Humvee and 105mm howitzer gun at 140 miles (225 kilometers) per hour.

Support Command

The Support Command Division provides the fuel and maintenance needed to keep aircraft flying. During an attack, the unit sets up a Forward Area Refueling Point (FARP) to keep the operation going.

The division has a complete field hospital. Its modified Blackhawk helicopters can carry up to six patients, and a 250-foot (76.3-meter) hoist can rescue troops or lift 600-pound loads. Humvees are used as ambulances to carry four to eight patients.

The division's fuel bladders can hold 500 gallons (1892 liters) of jet fuel. Portable generators transfer fuel from these bladders to filling stations for helicopters. Engineers use bulldozers to create landing zones and to build firing positions.

Air Assault

During an air assault, the first units of the 101st to land in new territory are the attack helicopters. Their job is to protect aircraft that are flying infantry to the target. Apache helicopters will defeat enemy resistance near the LZ (Landing Zone), and cover the transport helicopters as they land and depart. Apaches also protect Chinooks as they carry in cargo and fuel to the Forward Operating Base.

The timing of helicopters landing and taking off is important. A delay of a minute or two can throw off the whole operation. The landing zone must be chosen carefully so that helicopters and troops do not move into enemy fire. But the LZ must also be close enough to the objective to surprise the enemy. The division's skilled engineers must use maps and other information to choose the best LZ.

During an air assault, a lot takes place quickly in a short period of time. To make it work, each soldier must rely on self-sufficiency, coordination, and mental and physical toughness. The 101st Airborne offers a great challenge to those who want to be part of a hard-working team.

Glossary

Allies–friends of the U.S. in World War II

armed services–any branch of the military including the navy, army, Marines, and the air force

Armed Services Vocational Aptitude Battery (ASVAB)–a test taken before a person can enter one of the armed services

artillery–large guns and cannons capable of shooting long distances

basic training–the first training you experience when entering the armed forces

battery–a group of artillery pieces

battalion–a unit made up of four to six companies

brigade–a unit usually made up of 3 to 6 battalions, acting as part of a division

company–a unit of three or more platoons and including about 220 people

division–an army unit commonly made up of three battalions and smaller supporting units (battalions or companies). A general commands a division.

forward-looking infrared (FLIR)–the night vision used by aircraft that creates images from the heat given off by the target

infantry–the soldiers who battle on the ground and in direct contact with the enemy.

military entrance processing station (MEPS)–the place where enlistees take physical tests, pass a security check, and decide what career they want

platoon–a unit of three to four squads (40 to 50 soldiers)

recruiter–a military person who enlists new people into the armed services

regiment–a unit of three or four squadrons plus aviation

surface-to-air missile (SAM)–a missile fired at aircraft from the ground. Most SAMs can guide themselves toward the target.

To Learn More

Halberstadt, Hans. *Airborne: Assault from the Sky.* Novato, California: Presidio Press. 1989

Hole, Dorothy. *The Army and You.* New York: Crestwood House. 1993.

Kurtz, Henry I. *The U.S. Army.* Brookfield, Conn.: The Millbrook Press. 1993

Newsletter
The Screaming Eagle. The 101st Airborne Division Association, Sweetwater, TN

Videos
Airborne Assault (Command Vision, 1989)

Elite Forces: Paratroopers 1940-1945 (Castle/Lamancha, 1990)

46

Some Useful Addresses

**U.S. Military Entrance Processing
  Command**
2500 Green Bay Road
North Chicago, IL 60064-3094

The 101st Airborne Division Association
Screaming Eagle (Newsletter)
101 East Morris Street
Sweetwater, TN 37874

Don F. Pratt Museum
5702 Kentucky Avenue
Fort Campbell, KY 42223-5000

Reserve Officers' Training Core (ROTC)
Public Affairs Officer
U.S.A. Cadet Command
Building 56
Fort Monroe, VA 23651

Index